DESTINATION SPACE

WHAT ARE PLANETS?

David and Patricia Armentrout

A Crabtree Seedlings Book

CRABTREE
Publishing Company
www.crabtreebooks.com

Table of Contents

What Is a Planet?

Not all scientists agree on the definition of a **planet**, but many follow three rules.

Rule 1:

A planet is an object in space that **orbits**, or travels around, a star.

Rule 2:

A planet must be nearly round.

Rule 3:

A planet cannot share its orbit with a smaller object.

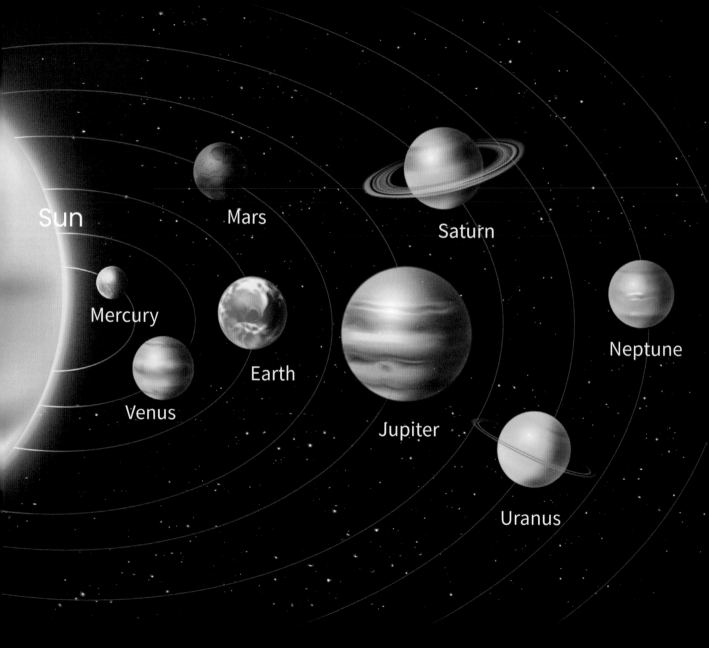

Sun

Mercury

Venus

Mars

Earth

Jupiter

Saturn

Uranus

Neptune

Following those rules, there are eight planets that orbit our Sun: Mercury, Venus, Earth, Mars, Jupiter, Saturn, Uranus, and Neptune.

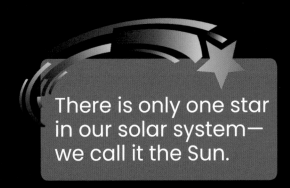

There is only one star in our solar system— we call it the Sun.

Sun

Mercury

Venus

Earth

Mars

Rocky Planets

Mercury, Venus, Earth, and Mars are the **terrestrial planets** in our **solar system**.

Jupiter   Saturn   Uranus   Neptune

Giant Planets

Jupiter, Saturn, Uranus, and Neptune are giant planets. Jupiter and Saturn are gas giants. They are mostly made up of gases.

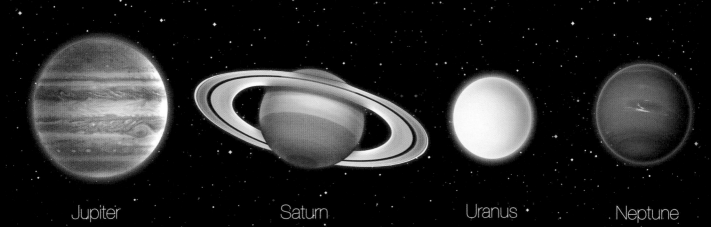

Jupiter   Saturn   Uranus   Neptune

Jupiter

Jupiter is the largest planet in our solar system. Its famous Great Red Spot is a storm that rotates counterclockwise.

Saturn

If you look through a telescope at Saturn,
you can see its rings. The rings are made
up of ice and rock.

Uranus

Uranus and Neptune are ice giants.
Their surfaces are mostly ice.

Neptune

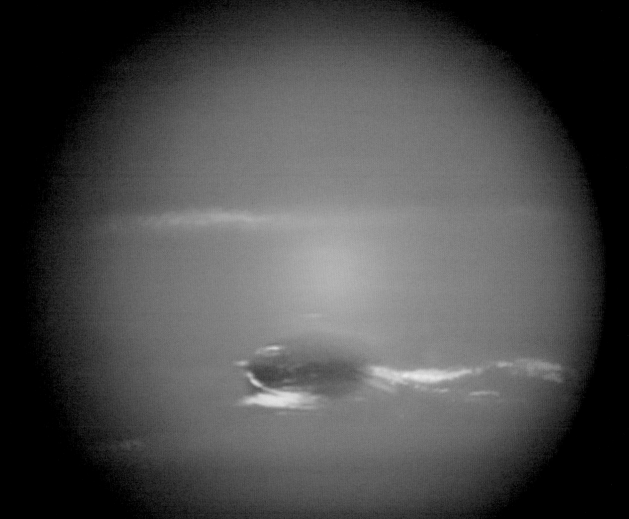

Of all the planets, Uranus gets the coldest, even though Neptune is the farthest from the Sun.

Sun

Mercury

Venus

Earth

Mars

Asteroid Belt

Jupiter

Saturn

Uranus

Neptune

Dwarf Planets

Beyond Neptune is the **Kuiper Belt**. It is home to several dwarf planets. Unlike a planet, a dwarf planet shares its orbit with smaller objects.

The Kuiper Belt is filled with icy objects left over from when the solar system was formed.

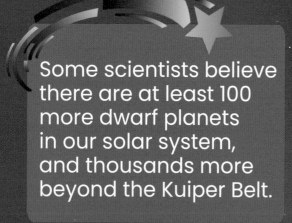

Some scientists believe there are at least 100 more dwarf planets in our solar system, and thousands more beyond the Kuiper Belt.

Pluto was once known as our ninth planet. In 2006, Pluto was grouped with other dwarf planets. That's because it shares its orbit with smaller objects in the Kuiper Belt.

Pluto

Exoplanets

An exoplanet is a planet that orbits a star outside our solar system. Scientists have found more than 3,000 exoplanets using land- and space-based telescopes.

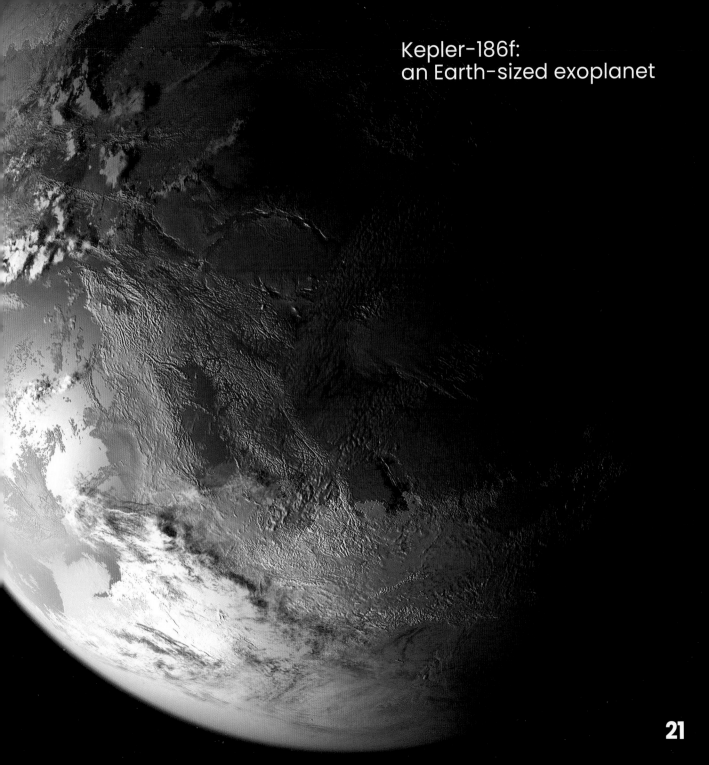

Kepler-186f:
an Earth-sized exoplanet

The Kepler observatory is a space-based telescope. With information gathered by Kepler, scientists were excited to discover an Earth-sized exoplanet that could support surface water.

Kepler observatory

Kepler and other space telescopes continue to help us explore beyond our solar system.

Glossary

Kuiper Belt (KY-per BELT): An area in space beyond Neptune that is home to icy objects such as dwarf planets and comets.

orbits (OR-bits): Travels in an invisible path around a larger object such as a planet or star.

planet (PLAN-et): An object in space that orbits a star.

solar system (SOH-lur SIS-tuhm): A group of planets, their moons, and other space objects orbiting a star.

terrestrial planets (TEH-res-tree-uhl PLAN-etz) Planets made up of mostly rock and metal; also known as rocky planets.

Index

School-to-Home Support for Caregivers and Teachers

This book helps children grow by letting them practice reading. Here are a few guiding questions to help the reader build his or her comprehension skills. Possible answers appear here in red.

Before Reading

- **What do I think this book is about?** I think this book is about the planets. I think this book is about the differences between planets.

- **What do I want to learn about this topic?** I want to learn more about planet Earth. I want to learn more about the rings around the planet Saturn.

During Reading

- **I wonder why...** I wonder why Uranus is the coldest planet, even though Neptune is the farthest from the Sun. I wonder why scientists keep looking for more planets.

- **What have I learned so far?** I have learned that a planet is an object in space that orbits a star. I have learned that the Kuiper Belt is an area beyond Neptune that is home to icy objects such as dwarf planets and comets.

After Reading

- **What details did I learn about this topic?** I have learned that Uranus and Neptune are ice giants. I have learned that Jupiter is the largest planet in our solar system.

- **Read the book again and look for the glossary words.** I see the word *planet* on page 4, and the words *solar system* on page 8. The other glossary words are found on page 23.

Library and Archives Canada Cataloguing in Publication

CIP available at Library and Archives Canada

Library of Congress Cataloging-in-Publication Data

CIP available at Library of Congress

Crabtree Publishing Company
www.crabtreebooks.com   1–800–387–7650

Written by: David and Patricia Armentrout
Production coordinator and Prepress technician: Tammy McGarr
Print coordinator: Katherine Berti

Print book version produced jointly with Blue Door Education in 2022

Printed in the U.S.A./CG20210915/012022

Published in the United States
Crabtree Publishing
347 Fifth Ave.
Suite 1402-145
New York, NY 10016

Published in Canada
Crabtree Publishing
616 Welland Ave.
St. Catharines, Ontario
L2M 5V6